INK ON PAPER

INK ON PAPER

Brad Cran

NIGHTWOOD EDITIONS

2013

Nightwood Editions
P.O. Box 1779
Gibsons, BC VON IVO
Canada
www.nightwoodeditions.com

Nightwood Editions acknowledges financial support from the Government of
Canada through the Canada Book Fund and the Canada Council for the Arts, and
from the Province of British Columbia through the British Columbia Arts Council
and the Book Publisher's Tax Credit.

This book has been produced on 100% post-consumer recycled, ancient-forest-free
paper, processed chlorine-free and printed with vegetable-based dyes.

COVER DESIGN: Brad Cran
TYPESETTING: Carleton Wilson

Printed and bound in Canada.

LIBRARY AND ARCHIVES CANADA CATALOGUING IN PUBLICATION

Cran, Brad, 1972–
Ink on paper / Brad Cran.

Poems.
ISBN 978-0-88971-281-2

I. Title.

PS8555.R3224I54 2013   C811'.6   C2012-908422-0

For Gillian, Rory and Micah.
And for Bruce and Linda Cran.

CONTENTS

Simple Music

IN PRAISE OF

FEMALE ATHLETES

WHO WERE TOLD NO

AND OTHER CIVIC POEMS

THIRTEEN WAYS OF LOOKING AT A GREY WHALE, ENDING WITH A LINE FROM RILKE

In recognition of two grey whales that swam into the harbour in downtown Vancouver in May and August of 2010.

1
An armoured lung,
a living castle of barnacle
and bone; a peaceful
leviathan moving with
the ease of a dark cloud.

2
The child knows more
about the grey whale
than the adult.

When given crayons
the adult says he does
not know how to draw.

The child is already drawing
the grey whale
with blue and pink.

3
In the world of opposites
the grey whale is an ocean cave
populated by sea otters.

4

No I didn't see the whale but
the man behind me at Starbucks did.
Everyone was talking about it
and someone said, "Did you
see the whale?" his eyes danced
and he shouted across the store
"I did," he kept saying. "I did.
I saw the whale."

5

And the whale said,
"Behold the natural world."

6

The woman died and the man
grew frail and ashen.
His life slowed to the pace
of the grey whale.

7

Forget the secrets of elephants.
The grey whale thinks in music.

8

In the Oregon aquarium, the children sit
below the skeleton of the grey whale
drinking cola.

9

The thing is, my dad doesn't like people much.
We saw the whale on the pier outside the market.

Even after the whale had gone, my dad wanted to stay
and talk to everyone else who had seen it.

10
Do not live in habit. Do not take the most
basic assumptions for granted. Consider
the city of whales. If you seek it with your eyes
you will never find it. It lives only in the symphonics
of the ocean. Its music is to the ear
as the pavement is to your foot.

11
Can you believe it's August. Can you believe
there is a whale in English Bay. How lucky
we are to walk through Stanley Park. My heart
beats at the speed of birds. I've stopped believing
in loneliness. Here we are. It's summer.
I want to be in love.

12
Some were trying to decipher
what the whale was telling us.
Others already knew.

13
And there you were
below the mountains
in the heart of the city
gazing at the grey whale.

You must change your life.

Are you bringing any fruits or vegetables into Canada?

Have you visited a farm in the last thirty days?

Are you now or have you ever been a member of a group that disagreed with government?

Do you intend to ride the zip-line?

Do you approve of product placement in movies?

Do you like my uniform?

Are you bringing into Canada any currency and/or monetary instruments of a value totalling CAD $10,000 or more per person?

Have you ever assaulted a police officer with a stapler?

In describing my uniform, would you say that it a) inspires respect or b) breeds contempt?

Have you ever dreamed of shooting a fascist dictator off a Spanish balcony?

Do you approve of John Furlong?

Can you give me an example of the words in your head and how they might be used while in Canada?

Do you vote?

Are you now or have you ever been a person who carries MasterCard?

Were you aware of the Oka uprising, and if so, whose side were you on?

Remind me again about the zip-line.

Do you read poetry?

Do you believe in homelessness as a right of the people?

If you were Canadian, and if it were possible to do so, would you vote
for John Furlong?

Does the colour of your socks match the colour of your pants?

Do your children own an effigy, stuffed or otherwise, of the Olympic
mascot?

Our premier rode the zip-line. Did you see that? It looks awesome.

Please arrange the following terms in order of preference, starting
with the least important: Health Care, Education, the Environment,
Homelessness, Logo Placement at Sporting Events.

Do you now or have you ever owned a copy of Raffi's *Baby Beluga*?

Do you own a cellphone?

Are you carrying any printed matter that illustrates same-sex love?

Are you bringing into Canada any firearms or other weapons?

What is the total monetary value of the goods you will be leaving in Canada?

Did you know that each year, more Canadians trust RBC Royal Bank® for their mortgage solutions than any other provider?

Let's go back to my uniform for a minute, you gotta admit it's pretty fucking awesome.

Do you or have you ever listened to *Democracy Now!*?

Can you finish the following sentence? Baby Beluga in the deep blue _____.

What colour is your heart?

Do you believe in global warming?

Have you ever purchased "No Name" brand products? You know, the ugly yellow ones?

If while in Canada you were Tasered, would you be upset or go into cardiac arrest?

Do you support an international unelected and roaming fourth tier of government as set out by a non-existent charter of the International Olympic Committee?

If your government acted against the principles of democracy, would you be compelled to action or would you just tell your friends you are miffed?

Do you ever experience emotions stronger than miffment?

If someone you knew spoke up against your government, would you a) listen or b) think that was a little weird?

When asked, will you keep the flow of traffic moving smoothly?

How long will you be staying?

AT THE VANCOUVER OLYMPICS I AM CANADIAN AND ON TV

British Columbia is super proud
To sing this welcome song,
For these wonderful Winter Olympic Games
We've awaited for so long.
 —From "Official Theme Song for the 2010 Vancouver Whistler Olympic
 Games (The Dead Children Were Worth It!)" by Geoff Berner

Past the street hockey game,
through the crowds and into
the thunder of nationalism,
I enter a pillow of light where I see
displayed before me the possibility
of television and the back
of Tamara Taggart's head.

And now I am on television,
hooting and jumping for my country.
That's me in the far right of the frame,
behind the back of Tamara Taggart's head.

I will run into the prairie of her hair.
I will take solace in her church.
I will cuddle the baby and invite
my friends for Pinot grigio.

Dance with me through the wheat.
Follow me to the creek. The priest
will apologize and the Prime Minister
will perch by the fireside and fill his heart
with the light of the locks flowing from
Tamara Taggart's head.

Send in the clowns and bring
an inflatable beaver.

How did the dancers get their jobs?
If only I'd known how to apply.

I sing from the diaphragm. I know all
the "Canadian" words to the anthem
but must admit I fake the French.

Now I could learn.
"This is the closest our country
has been since World War II."
J'imagine, j'imagine, j'imagine!

I wear our flag as a cape but I must leave the dream
of television and the back of Tamara Taggart's head
so I can urinate on a building.

I high-five strangers along the way.
Everyone is singing.

I shout the chorus and repeat the refrain.

Vous êtes un fouteur de cheval
et je ne suis pas un cheval.

I am trying to learn. Let me sing the solo.
Let me live in the dream and keep
the golden field, to forever drink
the promise of public love. I was on TV
and the Jumbotron, standing in front
of the back of Tamara Taggart's head.

It doesn't get any better than this.
Perhaps she will even turn around but right
now I am there, waving from the crowd.

I will count the pillars of our happiness.
I will thank our politicians. For this joy,
I will let them close a school.

AT LACY MADDEN'S GRAVE

for my great-grandfather Lacy Madden on the occasion of the rededication
of Mountain View Cemetery, July 10, 2009

At Lacy Madden's grave I'm thinking
about the Battle of Vimy Ridge and Hannah Montana,
the pop starlet my daughter dreams of in hues of burnt sugar
and sass. I don't know for sure if Lacy fought at Vimy
but I do know his regiment did and that he had left England
and arrived in Saskatoon only a few months before going to war
for this country that had just taken him in.

Lacy took a bullet and on the battlefield a surgeon
shortened his arm and drew him a picture of what he had done:
so as to explain things to the doctor back home.

Lacy came back from the war and moved west, where
he bought a piano on Granville Street from a store
that closed and became a mortuary. So here it is:
music and death and my daughter in my living room
pecking out Hannah Montana on Lacy Madden's piano.

Can you believe it? They were able to make pop music worse.

I'm trying to read the cemetery. I'm trying to forget *Poltergeist*,
zombie skin and the bitter Braille of horror's myopic blunders—
and the poor young men dressed as zombies who recently
showed up at the cemetery's public day, only to be greeted by
a Filipino choir and a lecture on Chinese burial rights.

How do we take death seriously?
How do we find the funniest person buried in the earth?

The men from the Second Narrows Bridge are in this ground.
The Chinese and Japanese coolies who built the railway. Joe Fortes
who himself must have kept dozens of people out of this cemetery.

I'm trying to imagine the cemetery as parchment.
I'm trying to see the punctuation and the minor story.
Harry Jerome crossing the finish line in '64 but also the man
in the crowd who watched him do it but whose memories
weren't preserved in the molasses of a bronze effigy—
and are instead kept in a shoebox to be sold at a garage sale
ten blocks south of here on some static Sunday.

Or imagine the veterans whose headstones sat atop rocks
and the men who pulled up these rocks and trucked them
down to Stanley Park to set them into the seawall.

Where do we connect with the past if not in these acres
of peace in the city? This park, the lavender and an infant stream
where marble text knocks our lives down to haiku and sunshine.

I'm thinking now of the importance of ritual
and whether we think we deserve it.

There is a rock garden in the heart of the cemetery
where parents can have the names of their lost babies
sandblasted into a stone, whereas until now each baby's life
had unceremoniously concluded with nothing more
than hospital protocol. How does a death
or a life change each stone?

A few years ago a man renovated the top floor of a house
in Toronto. He stripped and smashed the walls in and when
he found a package bundled in newspaper, it felt as light
as paper and he was sure he had found money but when
he cut the bundle open, he found a perfectly mummified
four-month-old baby, a little younger than one of his own children.

So after eighty years here was a stranger's grief
over a child that was fifty years his senior.

And here think of loss. Think of the mother in the twenties
who wrapped her child in newspaper and her husband
who plastered that child into the wall.

I'm thinking of ritual: of naming the world in sugar and salt;
of hearing the blood thunk of a collapsing bridge; of tapping out a tune
on Lacy Madden's piano; of seeing Harry Jerome cross the finish line
so fast that he turned to bronze; of remembering a child
who died so young no one knows her grave.

IN PRAISE OF FEMALE ATHLETES WHO WERE TOLD NO

*for the fifteen female ski jumpers petitioning to be included
in the 2010 Winter Olympics in Vancouver*

Despite the glory of colour it's easy to be the butterfly;
it's hard to be the dog or to remain like the river stone.
For Christ's sake, little lady, sit down you've been told.

Because he felt a woman short of breath was an affront
to good manners, Baron Pierre de Coubertin founded
the modern Olympics with only the strength of men in mind.
The heft and depth of sport could not be good
for the reproductive organs of a lady.
                            In 1896 at the first modern Olympics,
Stamata Revithi watched the men's marathon and the next day
started out on her own forty-kilometre run. She could not enter
the stadium to finish, as the men had done the previous day,
so with one lap around the entire perimeter she finished
the run thought impossible for a woman to complete.

The most unaesthetic sight the human eye could contemplate,
de Coubertin said, was women's sport. In 1922 Alice Milliat held
a women's Olympics in Paris where eighteen women broke
world records in sport. De Coubertin demanded that Milliat drop
the Olympic moniker from her games. She refused until
he promised to integrate ten women's events into the next Olympics.

De Coubertin added five female events to the 1928 Olympics
in Amsterdam. The Canadian women's relay team practised
by passing the baton on the deck of the ship that sailed them to Europe.
A contingent of Canadian men also travelled to Amsterdam,
to petition the IOC to drop female sport from the Olympics.

The media called the Canadian women's team "The Matchless Six."
The *New York Times* called Ethel Catherwood "the prettiest girl
of the Games," and the Saskatoon Lily for her "flower-like face."

It was said the Saskatoon Lily would become a movie star,
but Catherwood was an athlete. She said she would sooner gulp poison
than try her hand at pictures. She won gold in high jump,
still the only Canadian woman to win a solo gold in track and field.

That same year, women ran the 800-metre race so hard that when
they crossed the finish line they fell to the ground to catch their breath.
The men of the IOC found this disquieting. The 800 metre women's race
was not reinstated until 1968 in Mexico, where Enriqueta Basilio
became the first woman to light the Olympic cauldron.

Eva Dawes was a weak child and her father thought exercise
would strengthen her. He built her a high-jump pit at her school.
At a track meet in 1926 she won two gold medals in the under-
eighteen category. The officials refused to let her jump with the adults
until her father walked onto the pitch, grabbed the microphone
and pleaded with the crowd to intervene. The officials
let Dawes jump again and she won another gold that day.

In 1935 she wanted to see life outside Ontario, so she accepted
an invitation to travel to the Soviet Union. When she returned,
she was suspended from amateur sport for cavorting with communists.
The next year she boycotted the Nazi-hosted Olympic Games
and sailed for Barcelona to compete in the People's Olympiad,
championed by trade unions, socialists and communists,
and cancelled by the first shots of the Spanish Civil War.

Fanny Blankers-Koen gave birth to her second child,
immediately started training, and six weeks later competed
in the 1946 European Championships. By 1948 she'd held
many world records, but still the media thought she was
too old to represent her country, and should stay home
to take care of her children. She won four gold medals
at the 1948 Olympics. They called her the "Flying Housewife."

In 1973 former Wimbledon singles champion Bobby Riggs
claimed women didn't have the strength to play tennis properly,
and that he would beat any woman alive by virtue of his manhood.
He beat Margaret Court on Mother's Day of that year.

He said, "I want Billie Jean King. I want the women's lib leader!"
Riggs wore a *Men's Liberation* T-shirt to practise for the match
and claimed he wanted to be the number one chauvinist pig.

Rosie Casals called Riggs "an old man who walks like a duck,
can't see, can't hear and besides," she said, "he's an idiot."
Football players carried Billie Jean King into the Astrodome
while Bobby Riggs rode in on a chariot pulled by women.

Billie Jean King beat him three straight sets in a row.

Listen: here they come again,
trying to screw things up for the men. In 2005 Gian-Franco Kasper,
president of the International Ski Federation said:

"Ski jumping is just too dangerous for women.
It's not appropriate for ladies from a medical point of view."

The chivalry playbook? For the Continental Cup
in Germany the men's ski jumping team slept in a hotel
while the women were billeted in a farmhouse and barn,
with a pile of manure outside their window, and awoke to
a farm cat eating their food. Or they slept in a post office
in St. Moritz, or under a dining room table in Trondheim.

It is easy to be the butterfly. It is hard to sleep in the barn.

Perhaps your breasts are not aerodynamic. Perhaps jumpsuits
will increase the popularity of your sport. "Come here little darling,
and I'll teach you how to spread your V-style wider."

At the top of the cantilevered tower you envision yourself
in flight and prepare your body to react without thought.
You tighten the straps of your helmet, position your goggles,
slide onto the starting bar to watch the wind work the flags
with the possibility of flight as you slide your feet ahead
in the track, fold down and zip into the inrun—you feel
the compression of the curve. You are over the knoll.
                              If you bend your knees you lose control.
You master the airfoil and steer with the slightest movement
of your hands. You look straight ahead and command every turn
and nuance of posture. You are flying. There is no other explanation.

Your body is muscle and memory held up by the wind.

INK ON PAPER

THE ABACUS DREAMS OF UNREQUITED LOVE

Italics from "Daddy" by Sylvia Plath

Because daddy never loved my shiny beads,
the honest work I did
or because I was made obsolete.
And if I hate I hate Toshiba
money counters and greed,
the capitalists but the communists, too.
The poetry is the poetry is the poetry.
You do not do, you do not do.
Clickety-clack or energy in wire,
the calculation is to become.
I have little to say but more to prove.
You do not do, you do not do.
One day I will move my small hearts
of wood into the calculated dreams of the few
where with all of my life, *ich, ich, ich, ich.*
You do not do, you do not do.

In the fall of 2009 I was asked to support a collaborative project
in celebration of Chinese poet Gu Cheng, including a libretto he wrote
which would be set to music, along with a selection of his poems
that would be used as inspiration for contemporary Chinese rock songs.

Gu Cheng's poems move like slippery fish through the imagination.
His imagery is often built on an unexpected silver flash that seems
to make sense despite itself. The raindrops are minnows and you
must shut the windows before they swim inside to tickle your eyes.

The ethical problem of celebrating his playful poetics
comes from the time he spent in exile in New Zealand,
where Gu Cheng took an axe, murdered his wife, Xie Ye,
and then committed suicide.
                              I was told Gu Cheng's violence
could be explained by "the annihilation of self"
and "the collapse of the paradise garden."

It was important, I was told, that Gu Cheng's ghosts be exorcised
so his poems could be judged as the playful lyrics they were
intended to be, well before the tragedy. It was sad, I was told,
that the pressures of exile had killed Gu Cheng and Xie Ye.

I could accept the pressures of exile forcing Gu Cheng to suicide.
When it came to Xie Ye it was clear that exile didn't kill her;
the impact of Gu Cheng's axe did.

~

When Gu Cheng was a child, the Communist Party deemed
his family *bourgeois*. They were "sent down" to live as peasants
and raise pigs in the salt desert of Shandong Province.
Gu Cheng couldn't speak the dialect of the province and instead
immersed himself in what he called "nature's voice."
His first reading of a nature poem, he said, was a raindrop.

As a young boy, Gu Cheng held his father's hand
below a willow tree. He looked up and said:
"Losing an arm, I open wide an eye."
Gu Cheng was taken home where his sister taught him how
to draw the characters for the poem that would take its place
in his collected works as an early sign of prodigy.

The difference, I suppose, between a child prodigy
and the ubiquitous brilliance of children is Gu Cheng's words
were preserved. By the time he was twelve he would write
what would later become a poetic anthem for Chinese Poetry:

> *Even with these dark eyes, a gift of the dark night*
> *I go to seek the shining light.*

A child prodigy once paralyzed me with despair.
I must have been twenty-five years old and still struggling
to earn my first publications when I was introduced to
a twelve year old who played classical guitar in an orchestra.
His mother told me he spoke Spanish, which he'd insisted
on learning after discovering flamenco guitar.

He had read French philosophy, something I was then
sure I had to do—but really I was always unsure of myself
and writing was just a little dream I married to my latent instinct
to achieve meaningful work and quit smoking pot.

How can anyone compete with the life
of a bilingual child raised on brilliance and ego?

I received my first publication after a few more years—
but I felt greater peace when I heard the boy had given up
the guitar altogether. When I asked about the Spanish,
his mother insisted I must be thinking of another child.

~

In 1974 Gu Cheng moved back to Beijing,
where he worked in a factory and lived in what he called
"the light-filled crucible that melted down age-old humanity."
He befriended a group of poets who produced the magazine
Today. Their poetry rejected the social realism
used to lionize the heroes of the Cultural Revolution
in what Gu Cheng called "rhyming editorials."

By their choice these poets would have been called
the *Today* Group, but in denouncing Gu Cheng's poetry
a critic called him *menglong,* translating to *misty* or *hazy.*
In English they became known as the Misty Poets
and Gu Cheng became their most famous member.

The Misty Poets performed in stadiums packed with young people.
The Anti-Spiritual Pollution Campaign banned their poems.
Women chased them in public. "We swaggered through the streets,"
Gu Cheng wrote, "bullshitting and looking for a bathroom."

As a poet you don't need to be successful
to have success ruin you. What many young poets want
is the podium, sustained applause and a night of
marinated bocconcini at the Legion of Superheroes.

A poet from Ottawa told me he was sure to win
the Governor General's Award for becoming
the first person since Seymour Mayne
to publish three books in one year. It was clear
to him he simply couldn't be overlooked.

Sometimes we just swagger down the street
bullshitting and looking for a toilet.

❧

Gu Cheng met Xie Ye on a train
travelling from Shanghai to Beijing.

He wanted to live in an alternate world
of words with an unflinching dedication
to Taoism. In return he needed someone to
deal with the pragmatics of living a modern life.

He convinced her to drop out of school.
They married in 1983. On their wedding day
he said, "Let's commit suicide together."

❧

There are no gods of poetry;
there is only poetry itself.
I know this now. I didn't always.

Many poets write about goodness
because they see it as an essential

part of the craft. Marxism, for example,
can be worn like a coat.

Gu Cheng began the practice of cutting a leg off
a pair of trousers or blue jeans and fashioning it
into a hat that resembled a fez.

He told people he wore it so the ideas wouldn't escape
his head. He told people that at night he wore it
so he wouldn't lose his dreams.

I know of a poet who told his wife she should not talk
to him in the daytime while he was writing. Even if
he came out of his office to get a glass of water.
She should just ignore him and pretend he wasn't there
or surely an argument would ensue and then without
doubt his thoughts would be ruined.

At a dinner party Xie Ye said she wanted
to start recording Gu Cheng since she felt
every word he said should be preserved.

One of my most meaningful experiences as a writer
happened in an unlikely setting: a book awards dinner.
I sat with a woman from the Downtown Eastside—
a community whose women couldn't convince
the police they were being murdered, because
the majority of them were drug addicts and prostitutes.
By the time the police arrested the murderer, upwards
of forty women had been slaughtered.

The awards were over and another writer came to the table.
He started in on the sport of degrading the writers

who had happened to win awards. He gave a list
of who he thought was an asshole, whose books were shit
and then he was gone. That's when the woman
beside me said, "That man doesn't understand
how lucky he is that people listen to him."

~

Gu Cheng and Xie Ye moved to Auckland
so Gu Cheng could teach. After the Tiananmen Square
massacre it became clear they were in an indefinite state
of exile and they would not be returning to Beijing.

Gu Cheng taught conversational Chinese but did nothing
to instigate conversation with his students. They stopped
attending his class and, in turn, he was fired.

Gu Cheng refused to learn English.
He worried that the introduction of another language
would affect his ability to write poetry in Chinese.
Xie Ye negotiated the English-speaking world for him.

After they settled in New Zealand, Xie Ye
gave birth to their son Samuel. They bought a rundown house
on the island of Waiheke. On the first night
they placed their baby on the one sofa they owned
and lit a candle. Gu Cheng said it was the place he had
been looking for since he was twelve years old.
He wrote: "Listen, this house is our sunshine."

~

"The deepest of me," Gu Cheng wrote,
"has never been more than eight years old."

When Samuel was a toddler Gu Cheng kicked him
to the ground and Xei Ye promised Gu Cheng
she would take Samuel away, since Gu Cheng feared
he would hurt him again. Samuel was sent out of the house
and became a ward of a Maori woman who loved him.

There is a magic in the thoughts of children.
While growing up we let their brilliance
dissolve until there is nothing left
but a murky life of static thought.

If you want to worship poets then worship children.

I've asked adults to describe what they see
when they look at Picasso's *Guernica*—
a common answer is a confession
of not understanding modern art. I asked
a five year old to describe *Guernica* and she called it,
"the eye of pain which kills the horses."

In East Vancouver my wife and I asked a class
of six year olds to make a wish and write it down.
The smallest kid with the awkward handwriting wrote,
"I wish I saw a red cow in a dictionary."

I want to be six. I want to shut the eye of pain
and save the kingdom of horses. I want poetry to be
only what it is. I want to see a red cow in a dictionary.

~

Gu Cheng envisioned himself as patriarch
of his own childless harem he called "the Kingdom of Girls"
or "the dream of the Gu Cheng chamber."
In 1990 he arranged for a student who adored him
to immigrate to New Zealand.

Li Ying had been a beautiful and passive student
when Gu Cheng knew her in China but in New Zealand
she had clear desires of her own. She did not share a passion
for the rundown house that was Gu Cheng's "sunshine."

On the first night in the creaking house
Gu Cheng went to Li Ying and forced himself on her.
When Li Ying confided in his wife, Xie Ye asked her
why she thought she was brought to New Zealand.

Gu Cheng said that women are
only beautiful when they do nothing.

No matter how famous or critically acclaimed a poet gets
it is okay to completely dismiss his or her collected works.
Irving Layton said Wordsworth was turned on by daffodils
whereas Layton himself was turned on by "firm-titted women
walking on Avenue Road or St. Catherine Street."

I can accept Layton's passion for sex and women
but many of his poems taint his collected works
such as "Misunderstanding" in which he puts his hand
on a women's thigh—and by the way she pulls away
he concludes her devotion to literature is imperfect.

In my early days of writing poetry I had a friend who stood
by the poetry section of Munro's books in Victoria
in the hopes of meeting women. His pick-up line was,
"Do you like to read books because I like to write them."

He hadn't written any books then but he has now.
I hear he still brags about having multiple girlfriends.
He is happy with himself but never content with his career.
It would be unfair of me to read his poems. I hear they win prizes
but the better they are, the more inclined I'd be to hate them.

∽

Gu Cheng was offered a one-year position
in Germany that would pay enough money to renovate
the house on Waiheke. He told Xie Ye he would only go
if they could leave their child behind. The Maori woman
who took care of Samuel agreed but only if they signed
over guardianship to her. Xie Ye agreed. In Germany
she wrote to Samuel: "In the face of
such ugliness and suffering, my fragility
is no different from yours. How I wish you didn't know
such unbearable sadness in me. You have just turned
three and we have nothing but each other."

At a casual dinner party she told a person she'd just met
that she hoped Gu Cheng would die.
"I can't get my baby back" she said "unless he is dead."

∽

While Gu Cheng and Xie Ye lived in Berlin, Li Ying
eloped with a New Zealander, ending Gu Cheng's

"Kingdom of Women" fantasy. He became suicidal.
However misguided his vision of a harem, Gu Cheng
felt he needed to prove to Li Ying she was a fool
for throwing it all away. He set out to write the story
of the "Kingdom of Women." Xie Ye took another lover.

The book would be a testament to his love affair
with Li Ying and it would also be a plea for Xie Ye
to stay with him. To complete the book, he would
receive the highest cash advance in the history
of Chinese publishing. Xie Ye typed the manuscript.
Gu Cheng dictated the details of his love affair
and Xie Ye typed it all up. He was determined to make
Li Ying see how wrong she was to leave his kingdom.
At the same time he planned to make a lot of money.

He bragged that he could make Li Ying
moan in pleasure with the thrust of his hips.

While still in Berlin, Gu Cheng attacked Xie Ye
and nearly strangled her to death. She refused
to press charges against him and he was taken
to a mental hospital. He said his greatest happiness
would be if Xie Ye killed him. She continued to type
his manuscript. He dictated to her, "The minute
she leaves, then death has come for me."

❧

Back in New Zealand, Gu Cheng worried
that nobody loved him and that Xie Ye's lover
would move into the house he had built.
"Every nail in that house is a part of me," he said.

He would not let Xie Ye out of his sight
and even followed her into the bathroom.

Xie Ye wanted Gu Cheng to accept her lover
as she had accepted Li Ying but he refused
and told her that the situation was different
because different people were involved.

Gu Cheng went to Samuel's school and attempted
to take him out. He told the principal that he loved
his son and did not want Xie Ye to take him away.

Gu Cheng and Xie Ye agreed to divorce
but Xie Ye promised to not run off
and to continue to type his manuscript.

Gu Cheng agreed. He claimed
he was ready to learn English.

❧

It's hard to run the mathematics of tragedy
and come up with a mother's demise. After attacking
Xie Ye with the axe, Gu Cheng went inside
to wash his hands at the kitchen sink. He told his sister
he planned to commit suicide. He told her she should
not stop him as he prepared the rope he would use
to string himself up to a tree. His sister didn't know
what to do. Eventually she went to him and cut him
down but it was too late. Gu Cheng died before Xie Ye.

❧

Sometimes poetry bleeds from the flesh.
Other times it is just ink on paper.

Poet Pat Lowther said, "I think we are like a psychic
fourth estate, a conscious newspaper telling you what's
been happening inside your head while you weren't noticing."
I want to always believe this.

The best way to accept Gu Cheng is not as a poet
but as a child holding his father's hand below a willow tree
and thinking his first thoughts in the language of rain,
setting out to prove himself at the age of eight—already
collecting poems for his posthumous *Collected Works*.

How cute his pride and glory.

There he is hand in hand with his father.
There he is as any normal child wanting more in
the realm of *Why?* Pleased with possibility and pointing
toward the willow, "Losing an arm, I open wide an eye."

READING

READING AN AMERICAN MAGAZINE IN VIETNAM,
PERHAPS THE *NEW YORK TIMES MAGAZINE*
AND SOMETIME IN 1997

We were in love in Vietnam
and I had never been so jealous
of your French as the old men
came to you so excited
to hear you *parlez vous*
français. We were told the new
generation was only interested
in the language of money, English,
while French was the language
of love and poetry.

Women in the market carried
baskets of baguettes on their heads
instead of Asian vegetables. One was
asking about five cents per baguette.
When you gave her fifty by mistake,
she offered you every loaf she had.

We were told by other tourists
that Vietnam wasn't yet properly set up.
By that, they meant the country wasn't
fine-tuned for a tourist's enjoyment.
The pineapple sellers on the beach,
they said, were too aggressive.
When we went down there,
we saw that they were children
about eight years old. They showed us
pictures of their families

and asked for extra money and
for us to mail them some
particular item when we got home
but I can't remember
what that item was. I never ate
more pineapple in my life.

You were reading a magazine
the day we walked up the river
from Ho Chi Minh City.
You were disgusted and crying
over an article on female circumcision.
I'd never even heard of it before
and you had to convince me
it was real. You showed me the picture
of the Middle Eastern doctor
with a protruding Adam's apple
and a pencil-thin moustache who was
holding out a handkerchief
that had a women's clitoris on it.
There is no metaphor for this.
It still makes me sick.

On the bus to the Mekong Delta
a small American man in the seat next to me
said he had served in Vietnam.
His psychologist had suggested
he take the trip to help come to terms
with his time in combat. He said he was
told to talk about it openly but mostly
he just said "I've seen terrible things"
and "look at all this tourism."
I wanted to ask him questions

but I was too nervous. Later
he said you can ask me anything you like
so I asked him what it was like to serve
and he said, "I've seen terrible things."

We saw the Củ Chi tunnels.
I wouldn't go down them
but you did. I couldn't bear
the thought of being that closed in.

I suppose the worst thing we saw
in Vietnam were the deformities
caused by Agent Orange. In the American
War Crimes Museum we saw the jars
that contained the corpses of babies
whose bodies had been twisted by the chemical.

Tourism had never felt so strange.
That night we drank beer
outside at an open-air restaurant.

The next day we drank coffee,
set out on those French-style
silver platters we learned to love.
I'm still not sure if it is French
or Vietnamese style but it was
a perfect cup of coffee
with a little pot of condensed milk
and a long silver spoon.

Either way it was hard
to know what to make of the world.

Those deformed babies in glass jars
were what you wanted to talk about.
You insisted the missing tragedies
were the mothers' stories. The Museum
should have had some mention,
you said, of the mothers: what it was
like for them at the birth, the pain
of it all. How they probably wanted
to bury their children before
the doctors put each baby in a jar
and poured the formaldehyde in.

THE AVIAN FLU

My first recollection of the threat of avian flu
was in Tucson in 2002. Some friends
told me of a woman who had dedicated her life
to saving and rehabilitating raptors.
She lived on her own with little human contact
and prophesized a major culling of the human race
through an impending pandemic of avian flu.
It was not a matter of *if*, I was told she said, *but when.*

At times this woman's lack of human contact
became so extreme she'd invented a levered machine
that pressed two mattresses tightly together
so she could stand between them and pull the lever
in an attempt to emulate physical contact.
She had invented an apparatus that would give her a hug.

By all accounts she was not a cold woman:
she built her life on empathy of birds
but for the most part, I was told,
she had given up on humans.

Our daughter Rory turned one that year
and Gillian and I threw her a party
as well as one for ourselves. In the morning
we had her daycare friends to the house
and later in the afternoon we filled
our fridge with beer and hired a mariachi band
to play a set of songs. They gave us a discount
since we agreed to have them come early
in the evening. They arrived in a station wagon

wearing giant hats and matching green
mariachi *trajes*. We lived in a predominately Chicano
neighbourhood. Because of this, the band leader
predicted that when he played his trumpet
our neighbours would almost certainly consider it
an invitation to come over for a drink. Sure enough
he blew his trumpet and that night we met
our neighbours on both sides for the first time.

That was the same fall a disgruntled Gulf War veteran
flunked out of nursing school and walked into
the examination hall during midterm exams,
and in front of the other students he executed
three of his teachers, all of whom were mothers
of young children. He had enough ammunition
to kill hundreds of students but the police happened to
be nearby and arrived immediately, so the disgruntled
veteran turned the gun on himself and committed suicide.

It was days before Halloween. For fun,
some of the students wore costumes.
The shootings took place a few buildings away
from where we taught. For the first few days
no one said much. Gillian asked a friend about it
who said she felt bad for the mothers and their families
but just a year ago she had been living in Manhattan
and personally watched thousands of people die
in the World Trade Center, so it was now hard
to make a big deal out of three deaths
no matter how tragic they were.

It was Gillian who made a big deal about it
in our department. She asked me if she should say
something and I told her it wasn't our country
and nothing would change anyway. Gillian ignored
my advice and wrote an open letter. In it, she simply said
that three women had been killed on our campus
and it was insane no one was talking about it.

The following week the department brought in counsellors
to teach us how to deal with disturbed students,
how to evaluate the risk of violence and to discuss how
the shooting had impacted teachers across the campus.
People didn't know if it was their right to grieve.
They didn't know where to place their fear.

The bombing of Iraq also began that year. Rory went
to daycare at the Jewish Community Center.
When Bush enacted the Orange Alert, the JCC hired
security to monitor the parking lot and protect the daycare.
The guards wore orange t-shirts so people would know
they were there to protect the facility against the threat
of terrorism. Red, white and blue were the colours of
patriotism but orange became the colour of fear.

Fear beat in our chests like second hearts.

Word spread through the media
that the nuclear reactor in Phoenix
could possibly be a terrorist target:
all it would take to cause a meltdown
was one jihadist with a rocket launcher.
It seems silly now, but at the time it was hard not to
imagine the ease with which a nuclear explosion

could happen within a few hundred miles of Tucson.
We vowed not to let the gas tank in the car go below half
in case we needed to race toward California
and back up to Canada to escape the nuclear fallout.

At the JCC there was always one guard in an orange shirt
outside the daycare where a large cement wall separated
the parking lot from the playground. When I asked
about this I was told it was for the children's safety.
Then I was asked, *Do you know how easy
it would be to lob a grenade over that wall?*
By looking at the wall and its proximity to
the parking lot, it was hard to dispute that
yes, it would be easy to lob a grenade over that wall.

We accepted fear into our lives
with the ease of drinking water.

That year we watched news on the war
relentlessly. We followed every nuance
of American politics. When George W. Bush
defeated John Kerry we didn't leave the house
for days on account of a type of depression
I now suppose was really an extended bout of disbelief.
Kerry's concession speech ran on a loop in my mind:
"I wish things had turned out a little differently."

As a Canadian I suppose it is hard to know
if you should believe in bullets, grenades and bombs.
I have every reason not to, even while foreign wars
rage on. The children of those women who were murdered
are now a decade older and motherless.
The avian flu hasn't culled the human population yet but
the swine flu killed a few thousand people in 2009.

I do like plenty of quiet time but I don't care too much
for being alone. I suppose we are built to adapt,
to find ways to accept what we don't want to accept;
to look for comfort in small things, if need be.
A mariachi trumpet on your daughter's first birthday,
the friends who arrive with gifts and guacamole
and later sit down to tell you the story of a woman
who lives alone, rehabilitates birds and has invented
a machine to emulate the human embrace.

MORANS

Get a brain! Morans [sic]. Go USA.

—Text from protest signs of pro-war supporters engaged in a counter-protest against anti-war activists protesting outside the Boeing missile factory near St. Louis, Missouri, in March 2003

Pardon me your prison on the fourth of July,
your hee-hee talk and the ape of your heart.
From cattlemen to the county fair, even your
violence glows dumb. The spectacular left you—
now cellar to cellar your thoughts grow rot,
and no matter how many flowers may bloom
on top, there is no joy to see them in your hair.

You claim victories in the park but in fact
we grew tired of you and simply went home.
To say there was love between us is absurd.
Your despicable red sin, your happy gun,
your bravado under the calm broadcast of war.

You say that you will once again make America
number one. I say decades from now you will
look stupid even in your grave.

THE DEATH OF RONALD REAGAN: A FINAL
LOVE SONG

Nancy with your nights on fire,
let me be your cold wet rag.

My ghost will walk to the empty tomb
where I will wait for you to die.

When I met you in the middle
you became my everything.
The trumpets loose, the lips then purse
we walked to "Hail to the Chief."

Without you my life was wooden
then I loved you like sky,
like breath, like ocean.

How can I say it to you one last time?

I loved you more than I loved our own children.

PALIN'S JESUS

After Reading "Palin's Faith Is Linked to Form of Pentecostalism Known as Spiritual Warfare" by Laurie Goodstein, published in the New York Times *on October 25, 2008*

He will rise from the sea in sealskin and raven feather,
all Jordache and beauty pageant and keen for the next kill.
Now wolf and muskrat until the strength grows in his arms
and the heat of the fire is in his hands and pumping the blood
through his American heart. Fuck Bethlehem. We shall ride
the Iron Dog along the Bering sea. *Oh Sarah sit with me awhile—*
I will count the peaches on your breath and share
your sweet cider as we plan our ride into the depths
of their Armageddon. Even their birds will pay.

We must go back to the founders, Palin says, *and I mean*
the founding documents that are clear in their understanding
of creation and the ability of ourselves to know what it is
to be in support of the Judeo-Christian basis of American Law.

But Palin's Jesus doesn't give a shit; and she likes that.
Buck up or stay in the truck and they are skidooing through
the fields of snow and down the Yukon River so that he
may kick the doors open and enlist with a signature in blood.

Bless the American soldiers. Bless the fear of God.
Bless the $30 billion gas pipeline that will require
God to unify the people and the companies to
"get this thing done." Pray for a speedy end.

On September 11 Palin's Jesus will deploy with her son
while Sarah sings in the media tent, does a walk past
in bikini and sash. She will answer the question on world peace,
and say Jesus is her role model. We can see our Sarah score.
The red carpet is unfurled. We can see the Russian shore.
From the beaches of Alaska we can smell the end of the world.

READING WITTGENSTEIN

I was reading Wittgenstein when
all three were killed on the viaduct.

A picture shrine and flowers
on three of the four corners
at the intersection by my house.

When the phone rang I was alone
in a small room. There is a bill
I cannot pay. Even when my eyes burn
I do not turn off the television.
I am also reading Wittgenstein.
Blue light fills my mind
and in walks Ludwig Wittgenstein.
Wittgenstein, how to make sense of death
and intertwine Ludwig Wittgenstein?

And now I'm driving or phoning.
At least always driving and planning
on driving and turning toward the viaduct,
and reaching for the phone and cocking it
between my ear and shoulder
and looking and changing lanes,
getting across and moving toward
an exit. And I use my horn
on these poor sods who can get out
of the way of nothing. O Nothing,
and my poor dead Ludwig Wittgenstein.

I'm thinking about driving
into Ludwig Wittgenstein
and through his beautiful mind.
And I shall paint the walls
in primary colours
and as my car disappears
it will be clear I fly on—
gentle through the fields
of Ludwig Wittgenstein.

Dear Wittgenstein, kiss me home
and tell me how to make sense
of the viaduct, the lotus field
and the flicker of blue
in my small room.

I love you, my idea
of Ludwig Wittgenstein.

People like ants
disassemble the viaduct.
There is a song
being composed on guitar.
There is a photograph
in the newspaper
and the headline reads:
"Family killed on the viaduct."
                    I'm driving through the city
and toward their hometown,
north toward the trees and light.
In my mind there is an epiphany
I'm trying to remember
about the relationship between nature

and the thoughts of Wittgenstein
but all I remember is that it was
as beautiful as rain, or the idea of rain,
as one drives through the snapping
of epiphany brought by Wittgenstein.

The song will be sung,
and will jingle through the minds
of mourners, public and private.
For this death, I will be both,
driving toward their hometown
and also in the grocery line
publicly staring at their portrait
in the paper. I will gather butter
and olives. Cream for my skin.
I will smell the fire-roasted pepper
and I will taste cheese from the goat.
At home I will recycle the paper.
I will move to the living room
and reread my notes on Wittgenstein.
I will sing the song and make sense
of the viaduct. I will take gin in a plastic cup.

A SWIMMING POOL

In the Comments section of the *Globe and Mail*
the man from Alberta who calls himself "Truth Be Told"
wrote that he was sick and tired of the whiny crackheads
who think it's the world's fault they are losers
and he hopes the money allocated to fixing up
Vancouver for the Olympics will include funds for a barge
so all the crackheads in the city could be put on it
and towed out to the Pacific Ocean.

If you go down to "the bad side of town" in summertime
and ask a crackhead what the neighbourhood really needs,
there is a 95% chance you will hear "a swimming pool."
The same goes for heroin addicts, prostitutes,
drug dealers, part-time construction workers,
social workers, hotel desk clerks, pizza delivery people,
entrepreneurs, librarians, healthcare providers,
and anyone else you may see on "the bad side of town."

What you will hear as every answer will be:
swimming pool, swimming pool, swimming pool.

If you then go to the other side of town, which is to say
"the good side of town" by most accounts, and tell
people at a public swimming pool that a poor person,
who happens to be a crack addict, thinks a swimming pool
would be just what "the bad side of town" needs,
there is a 95% chance these people won't believe
an idea so preposterous could be suggested
with any seriousness. After all, they will say,
who would swim there?

FUN-LOVING NICKLEBACK POLICY MACHINE (WITH KITTENS)

In response to John Ibbitson's October 14, 2011, Globe and Mail *column*
"The alarming decline in voter turnout."

Sweater vests can be made in Canada but
more likely you wear one from Bangladesh.

In picking kittens remember tabbies are best.
Avoid regal cats and expensive galas that
cost more if you fly in on one of the jets.

Remember that politics is the art of grey
and it's okay to win by saying nothing.

Keep yourself in check or one day you will
ride the lakes of your ego on a Jet Ski.

Failure is easy to come by and you can find it
in simple things. Ignatieff couldn't eat a cracker
without looking like a scion who was born to fix
the world. Thumbs-up and seal meat, ready to sing
Springsteen to a Nickleback crowd. Rise up indeed.

The past is best forgotten. Remember, black and white
photography was too kind. No politician alive could
survive Trudeau's dive or pirouette in the age of viral.

The week Jack Layton died, rest in peace, a friend of mine
said while having a bad day he sat down with
a coffee and thought, "What would Jack do?"

God help us. Even the righteous
are reduced to a Timbit slogan.

I'm reminded of something the songwriter
Rodney DeCroo once said to me in jest:
"I'm an independent thinker—I read Chomsky."

How do politicians take a stand on issues
if all we do is send them onto *The Dating Game?*

Thirty-four million people and we believe there
is only one choice for the top job?

Your personality awaits. It's you in grey.
People will stand when you enter the room.
You will fly Super Elite. And when you run
through the airport they will say, "There she goes."

If you are bland as glue then give it some zip
but avoid the issues you know won't stick.
The important thing is to give Canadians
what they want: Yo-Yo Ma and "With a Little Help
from My Friends," a fun-loving Nickleback
policy machine and for good measure throw in
some kittens. Live in the world of *seems.*

After all, Ignatieff was right when he said that in politics
people are only interested in what you have said
and have little interest in what you mean.

HANDS AND PIXELS

After reading "The Case for Working With Your Hands" by Matthew B.
Crawford in the New York Times

Of all the past things, I'd advocate for birds and sleep
by the Vedder River, in the meadow a carving stone itself
whittled into a bone. To make something with your hands
or to ride on illusion and mill nothing out of the trees?
Speculation dehydrates the soul as we pour ourselves gelatinous
into the Zuckermould. Archive and backup.
Zip, compress, send and repeat. We are dreaming
in a forest without an axe. To sleep in productivity
and awake in a spreadsheet. To burn your retina
and then relax. To breathe stale air and let your mind
drink pixels. To think you are thinking deeper, going on:
for and against the modern world.

FACEBOOK

Now that you speak in roses and snake tongues.

Now that you dream of poison apples.

Now that they have actually invented
something that is worse for writers
than alcohol.

Now that your ego is a podium
that you have carved out of pixels.

Now that everyone understands
your outrage over the federal budget,
even though you have not read
the federal budget.

Now that you have had a cappuccino.

Now that the Coffee Barn has the best froth.

Now that you were the first person
to know about the singing cat,
the drunk baby, and the father
who built his three year old
a backyard rollercoaster
out of PVC tubing.

Now that you are confused about the lack
of love in your life, while you grapple

with the uncertainty between the PVC
rollercoaster being an act of love or abuse.

Now that you signed the petition.

Now that it is "such sad news"
that Phyllis Diller died
in her sleep at age ninety-five.

Now that you "liked" the Che Guevara
fanpage even though it turned out to be
an advertisement for the Che Guevara
energy drink.

Now that you have felt betrayed
and attempted to get to the bottom
of this Che Guevara energy drink.

Now that you believe Putin somehow
cares what you think about Pussy Riot.

Now that you sit in your own backyard
and throw eggs at a stone wall.

Now that you think in the way
Zuckerberg said you would.

Now that you have 1,347 Friends.

Now that you read fewer books
(yes you do.)

Now that you update your status
from your mobile device and because
of this you almost missed the kiss
at your own wedding.

Now that you frustrate your enemies
by "liking" them.

Now that metaphorically speaking
you are a fascist general who escaped
an assassination attempt by abandoning
his own children and making a break for it
through the booby-trapped olive grove.

Now that you will be the first to turn
on Pussy Riot when, metaphorically speaking,
they sell the rights to their own energy drink.

Now that your eyes are broken glass.

Now that you still enjoy sex with a person
but on most days are happy to make love
to pixels and ejaculate into your T-shirt.

Now that you speak to yourself. Now
that you speak to yourself. Now that
you speak to yourself.

Now that your mind won't turn off.

Now that your mind is a subordinate
conjunction desperately searching
for its clause.

SIMPLE MUSIC

CONFLATING MEMORIES WHILE LISTENING TO "DAY IN, DAY OUT" BY BILLIE HOLIDAY

In the Rome of my youth I wore a paper hat.
They said bebop and I new what they meant,
danced the foxtrot and called my friends "buster."

But a year later I fished steelhead, ate mud
and slept on the banks of the Vedder.

We drank vodka called Silent Sam,
no more smokes on the drive
back down the valley, which in all respects
is a highway to everywhere.

The music purred, then bounced.

I quit my job to watch a man play guitar.

Of all the stupid fucks I hope I was at least
the stupidest for a night or two.

At sunset when my friends jumped off
the cliff and into the lake, I was the one who
instead scuttled down like a drunk spider.

I always loved the drive back down the Hope–Princeton.

You can see a pioneer still waiting to walk out
of his life and into Technicolor.

It didn't matter where we were going
but we were going to the rhythm of Art Blakey.

I also liked Lester Young and Horace Silver
but I forget them now.

Above all my grandfather liked the music
of Tex Beneke and Glenn Miller.

At university we listened to Herbie Hancock
playing "Cantaloupe Island" over and over.

Then the remix with Pee Wee Marquette.

I danced with two women
in my living room and one asked me
to take a bath but I did not understand
until later that if I had said yes
that this could have lead to sex.

Instead I declined and danced into my own head
to the music of a blue trombone.

Truth is okay but I prefer the crack
and pepper of a flawed memory.

There are two things that remind me of sex:
the sound of a saxophone and the scent of mock orange.

I am with you in Tucson walking the warm street
and there is something else I am remembering.

You are now in the memories I formed before we met.
I love that I've gotten it all wrong.

Surely we were walking down that street but
doesn't it feel more accurate to say that we were dancing?

Memory is the most imperfect journalism
but I can tell you: mostly I'm the one who is right.

I remember clearly now, how to hold you
with the arrogance of youth.

Somewhere encoded in my mind, is that jazz.

THINKING OF THAT BAR IN THE BASEMENT OF
THAT BUILDING WHERE WE USED TO GO

for Adam Chiles

After all these years it seems like I'm looking
for a friend. The centre of being. The refrigerator
is broken and I've said fuck it and gone to the pub.
I've locked myself out of the house and I'm sitting
on the porch. I've had a fight with my wife
and I don't know where to go.

I suppose I'm looking for you and by that I mean
I'm looking for the person I am when I'm around you.
That centre of being. I want to be stupid with you.
I want to lose time in the basement of that building
where we used to sit so many years ago. I believe
we were talking about the possibility of trains
and the logic of laughter.

I'm not sure where the bartender is
or whether we've even paid the bill.
You reach for your coat, and simply put:
I'm following. You see my friend,
even these days alone I'm right behind you.

CONTEMPLATING DIVORCE WHILE WATCHING PORN AT THE LOCAL BEST WESTERN TWO MILES FROM HOME

I feel displaced by hotels.

I want the illusion of luxury yet here I sit against bad art,
corrugated wallpaper and a television that proffers
nothing more appealing than unlimited pornography
between now and noon for $19.99.

When I leave I will take the small bottle of shampoo.

And now I sit to watch the gorgeous of the world having sex.

On the television a beautiful woman presents herself
and says she wants to suck a cock.

My wife doesn't understand me.

Now this woman is saying it again and again with such
vigour that I don't believe her. A nameless man walks
on screen and I'm reminded of a modern proverb:
"Never fall in love with a waitress.
They are paid to be nice to you."

Surely this woman's desire is dangerous as she screams
to me through the San Fernando Valley, and into my little
room in the Best Western two miles from home.

Now the nameless man calls the woman a "sexy bitch."
Misogyny is the cardinal sin of pornography.

For once why couldn't the nameless man say:

"The stars are blue,
and without you
there is ice in my heart."

I love my wife and when I return I will give
her the small bottle of shampoo.

The man's penis goes everywhere in the woman's body
at least twice and rather than being turned on
I want her to stop and brush her teeth.

I want to know if the hotel manager approves.

I may feel like the pervert who rented this movie
but more accurately, the hotel manager
is the pervert who rented it to me.

I will take the small bottle of shampoo and the bar of kiwi soap.

How can we talk about desire? How can we break away
from the domestic life and look to be anything
but maliciously horny? How quickly desire turns toxic
when we talk about it with public honesty.

To be fair, I could never handle my friends talking graphically
about sex. A friend from university had a threesome
and wrote to me describing his experience in exact detail.
I had thought of him as an intellectual equal but was then
confronted by his metaphor "pussy sandwich," as in
"my girlfriend got on top of her and I ate a pussy sandwich."

Sex overtook him. He came to me with great urgency
to ask if my girlfriend and I would like to join an orgy.
I politely (how else) declined. He was visibly upset and
told me to look him in the eyes and swear that I didn't
want to watch his girlfriend eat my girlfriend's pussy.

No, I just honestly really didn't.

I would guess most of the men and women in porn
are in their mid-twenties but even now I can't help
but think of them as being older than I am. Sex still
seems to be for a maturity I'm striving to obtain.

Sex had innocence when I was innocent.
My official sex education was doled out in one class
in grade five by an overweight physical education teacher,
who told us that the term boner was incorrect since penises
do not contain bones.

My eldest daughter was taught sex education in preschool
at the age of four. The thinking behind this is that you are
never too young to have the ability to understand and
protect your own body. Of course I agreed.

After our second daughter was conceived
I asked my eldest if she intended to help
with the coming baby. She said she would
like to help but she would not change any diapers.
When I asked her what she would do, she told me
that she'd help me put the sperm in.

The first causality of divorce is your collective memory.
The inside joke and the day-by-day rote love. The joy

of dreaming about divorce is the momentary escape
from domestic limbo. *I will be human again. I will
sleep. I will have desire.* My wife and I both thought
that we needed a divorce but under the fog of sleep
deprivation it turns out all we needed was a nap.

When confronted by love, hate dissipates.
The phone rings and I want her back. I want her
teeth against my skin. I want her to come for me
in the Best Western two miles from home.
I want her to come for me from the San Fernando Valley.
I want her to throw me against the corrugated wallpaper
and dig her fingernails into my back. I want her breath
in my ear.

*I love you my darling.
I am sorry, too.*

*The stars are blue,
and without you
there is ice in my heart.*

Come to me my love, come to me with flowers
in your hair. Come to me with your skin flush red.
Come quickly. Come now.
The kids can play in the pool.

SCIENCE FICTION

In writing school we were all so in love with ourselves
that we wanted to be someone else, someone good enough
to reflect our egos back to us in pleasing ways.

We had a Gwendolyn MacEwen type, who had windswept eyes
and a penchant for rowboats that she would fill with candles
and use to sail out of the classroom and down the street
in a funeral procession led by her own mother's hate.

We had a Paul Theroux who would never shut up.

I suppose at the time I wanted to be Raymond Carver.

But of all my classmates the person I remember clearest
was the one everyone respected the least: the small awkward
student who wrote science fiction.

He was perhaps the most passionate person in the class
but his passion for science fiction made him even more absurd
to a group of young people already dreaming
about the composition of their literary obituaries.

To introduce a story he said:

*What you need to know is that there are three moons
that revolve around the planet of Andor.*

Then he was gone into the science of his plot: the effect
of the gravitational pull on character development,
the available ballistics, how they'd have guns

but preferred to fight with sabres and his hero who shall,
by the end of his story, slaughter the orc-like villains
and send them back to a life buried in clay.

His work was widely dismissed.

He was given suggested readings:
serious books by serious authors.

He came back to the next class
with a poem he had written about karate.

He stood up, took off his coat and from his bag he unfolded,
and then put on, a white karate jacket, which in all honesty
made him look even smaller.

He squared his feet back, braced his body in battle position
and shouted his poem while punching the air.

He may have even have had good style but the sight
of this tiny science fiction writer, dressed for karate
and punching his poem into being, was simply too much
for our group to handle. When those who were trying to
hold back their laughter simply could not anymore
it blew out of our chests uncontrollably until
everyone was openly laughing.

He simply stopped, picked up his jacket,
walked out of the room and never came back.

Officially we were told that he had dropped the course
to find something that was "a better fit."
Unofficially we talked about "the moons of Andor,"

his karate position and whether or not he was the kind
of person who would come to our class and shoot everyone.

At that time, in our early twenties, we just couldn't see past
our own self-delusion, but in thinking about him now,
I understand he was just a young man
who desperately wanted to make himself stronger.

We were all so wrong about science fiction.

Three times in my life, in very real ways, I have felt
the knowledge that I have super powers. You see, one day
I became a super villain and had the power
to shoot beams of energy from my chest.

I have also glimpsed portals
and occasionally I can see through them.
Lastly, when certain elements line up with my body,
I gain the perception of perpetual speed and I do indeed
become the Flash, the fastest man in the world.

On April 17, 2007 at approximately 5:14 pm in front of my house
my daughter, age five, waved at a friend from the sidewalk.
When she stepped off the curb and ran to go see him,
a speeding SUV struck her and knocked her down the street.

I saw the impact from our living room window.
I may have flown off the front of my steps.
I may have teleported to her.

I can't be sure how I got there,
but when I picked her up
blood trickled out of her mouth

and I went into shock.

As it turned out, the blood from her mouth was not
internal bleeding but ran from a deep cut
where she bit through her tongue.

Three ambulances and two fire trucks came.

She had muscle pain and road rash up one side of her body
but otherwise was fine. Gillian held her and I went outside
where the driver of the SUV was in our front yard
with her camera. She was taking pictures of the street
and her vehicle. She kept repeating to my neighbour
that she wasn't going to have to pay.

This is when I became the super villain.
As clearly as I have the power to walk,
I could feel the hate in my chest coagulating
into a ball of energy that I was sure I could shoot
from my chest to vaporize her.

I could feel the power to kill her
through the strength of my hate.

I charged at her and my neighbour intervened.

I thought about releasing a beam of hate
and vaporizing them both but instead I told her
to leave my neighbourhood or I would kill her with my bare hands.
My neighbour insisted that she stay until the police arrived
and I went back inside to get Gillian because I was certain
Gillian would want me to kill her—but instead
she told me to calm down. I couldn't understand her.

A police officer came in to check on Rory and question us.
Gillian started by apologizing for me and telling the officer
I was just upset. She told him about the woman taking pictures.
The police officer said he would have been equally angry
but we should keep in mind "the driver of the vehicle
was in shock." I said, yes I was sorry, that I got caught
in the heat of the moment, that I was just worried
about my daughter. But really I was lying to them
and I wanted them to believe me so I could leave
and follow the woman home, because even then
I still wanted to kill her.

Gillian began to cook. I usually do the cooking
in the house but in this moment she began to cook
and cook and cook. She could not stop cooking.
Her mood was jovial which frustrated me because
I wanted to convince her that we should burn the world.
She invited the police to stay. She would make pineapple
and red pepper shish kebabs, with a teriyaki glaze.
Garlic mashed potatoes and all of Rory's favourite food.
There would be enough for the ambulance drivers
and all the neighbours. Really they should all stay.

It was as if the accident had cheered her up.
It wasn't until three months later that her hair
began to fall out. At first we noticed just a little,
but then it became clear that her beautiful hair
was falling out in large clumps.

We took her to the walk-in clinic and the doctor
asked her if she had suffered a trauma within the past
few months and she told him, *Three months ago,*

if only for a moment, we thought we were going
to lose our daughter.

That fall Gillian and I finished collecting oral histories
for a book called *Hope in Shadows*. We would take turns
going to the Downtown Eastside to interview
disadvantaged people about their lives. We alternated
so neither would have to take the full emotional burden
of hearing stories of abuse that are so common
in an impoverished neighbourhood.

Sometimes the stories would inspire us, but often they
would open us up to a narrative we weren't
always prepared to hear. One day I listened to the story
of a woman I assumed was about forty years old.
She had started working as a prostitute at the age
of thirteen. She was in a wheelchair because someone
had thrown her down the escalator at the Granville SkyTrain
and one of the striped metal steps crushed her vertebrae.
Recently she had been panhandling outside the Roxy
nightclub and some men came out of the bar
and threw her out of her wheelchair. I asked her age
and found out she was actually twenty-four years old.

When I got home I had two goals: to keep calm
in front of my kids and drink as much wine as possible.
I must have poured half a bottle into my first glass.
I prepared myself to put up with my kids' misbehaviour;
I would do everything I could to hold it together,
but Rory could tell something was wrong.
She hugged my legs and said, *Daddy, you're the best daddy*
in the world. And that is what set me off, bawling
like a child in front of my own children.

Sometime that fall, my friend Ian introduced us
to the music of Jonathan Richman. I wasn't familiar
with Richman's music but Ian had tickets to see him
and he assured us we'd love his show. So we went.

I now own many of his albums but it is Richman's
Rockin' and Romance that became an important part
of our lives. This album is a sonata to happiness.
It is sunshine and beach sand. It is the human condition
told through the quest for a new pair of jeans.

On days we had hard interviews it was our cure,
our cleanser: to go for a run and listen to *Rockin' and Romance.*

Three years later the book was going into a second printing
and I was at my publisher's. He said he had forgotten
to tell me but we had received a letter. It was a letter from
Jonathan Richman. He wanted us to know
that he had been in town performing and a homeless person
had sold him a copy of *Hope in Shadows.* He was writing
to say how much he enjoyed it. This was more important
than just receiving a note from someone we admired.
It was a convergence. I couldn't have been on my bicycle
fast enough. I was peddling as quickly as I could.

I had to get home to show Gillian
this letter from Jonathan Richman.

I was biking down Abbott toward BC Place
and the road was blocked. People were standing around.

There was a baby stroller in the street under a yellow tarp.

I asked someone what had happened and was told
a mother was waiting at the light to cross the street,
and when she stepped off the curb a tow truck hit
and killed her baby.

Panic set in. Again I couldn't get home fast enough.
I needed to get home as quick as possible.
Every molecule of my body was water.
It was as if I could slip into the ocean.

This is how it happens. A mother's life
changes forever one afternoon.
Where could that mother place herself
after such a horrible loss.

Sometimes all we have is fantasy.
Sometimes we need science fiction.

Throughout the city you can see memorials
built for people who have been killed by motorists.
Each memorial has its own distinct energy.
The memorials with the strongest pull
are the two I have seen in the city
that were erected for children.

One is framed around a teddy bear
tied to a pole with purple ribbon.

The other is a perpetually refreshed stack of flowers
above a large Tonka truck.

I haven't yet figured the science out, how exactly they work
but I believe they are portholes to a second chance,
an alternate universe or a world with different gravity.

What you need to know is that there are three moons
that revolve around the planet of Andor.

From a hundred yards back of a roadside shrine,
I can spot the flicker of another world, the glimmer
of something as easy as a second chance. As I get closer
the portal fully opens; a child is again standing
by the road, everything depends on this. I am the Flash.
My thoughts are lighting, my heart beats
by its thunder. The child fidgets and I am running.

NORMAL

For my daughters Micah-Sophia and Rory Sarah

I'm fighting normal. I'm choreographing
this other dance, where you spin across
the floor and out the door while the other
kids are still jumping on the spot, popping up
to learn ballet. From an outsider's eye,

you might call ours the dancing raccoon disco,
or perhaps we are the hip hop squirrel brigade.
The slippery salmon lovers of clouds? Or are we
the bears who hold up signs saying, *Will work
for honey and funk!* Find your totem.

There is no tradition I will hold you to.

What I'm saying is that I want you to keep moving
and I don't care if it is in your body or your mind.

When the other kids pirouette, you are already
gone. You've sold your tutu and moved to Amsterdam.
You have woken on a beach in Vanuatu
and when the person you love says, *I love you,*
you have the confidence to say, *I love me too
and that's why I can love you back
ferociously in the language of red.*

It's simple really: I want to give you both the gift of *yes.*

The door is open and even though we are supposed to stay,
we are spinning across the floor
in violation of expectation and structure.

What I'm saying is: go barefoot. Or walk out
with a handstand. Live in possibility
and in constant proximity to desire.

Don't just dream; burn your dreams.
Heat your life with that fire.

HISTORIES

We can date your hurt back through the history
of the Catholic Church and the hypocrisy
of annulments and the priests taking care of their own,
until one day history would bloom in your life,
and suddenly the sugar bush was gone,
your house sold to split equity
into a million shards of pain.

Although I've never set foot on an ocean liner
I trace my hurt back to a lone Scot bound
for Australia to sire a son who would grow up
to abandon my father. It was the hard life
of the determined immigrant, sure to be
the last vulnerable son. How sad that they all
looked to money to block their fear.

In some ways we are all children
coming to terms with history.

How bad do we have it?
How bad did they have it?

Our friend's mother fled Eastern Europe
from some dire camp—which is to us
a type of fiction but to him was a childhood
of boxed ears and smacks on the head.

Your great-grandmother seemed stuck
in the time of pioneers until she abandoned
her family to follow racehorses and a young
lover to Cuba. I suppose I can't blame her
but I wonder now how her disappearance
fell down into your life through a fist or a kiss.

Our friend's mother keeps everything she needs in life
packed tightly in a suitcase. It has been sixty years since
she fled but she's still packed and ready to go.

Apparently I had a great uncle who didn't even
like the idea of a suitcase and when he left on a trip
he wore two sets of clothes and took one set off
when he arrived at wherever it was he needed to be.

How quick we are to cut ourselves off from our histories,
to assign our disappointment to our parents, messengers really.

And perhaps our love was at first a type of forgetting.
We were so eager to write our own history. I'm so thankful
it began in something as silly as a blue Volvo
you had named Betsy. We were so in love we barely ate.
Instead we were sated by our own company and pulling
over at that highway gas station for a fistful of red licorice.
We shared it in the parking lot with the windows down
so we could enjoy the bliss of summer wind, which
I realize now was also just the simple music of our lives.

NOTES AND ACKNOWLEDGMENTS

Thank you to the Canada Council for the Arts and the BC Arts Council for their support which enabled me to finish this book. Thank you to my editor Silas White for his superb editorial work. Thank you also to Steven Price, Srikanth Reddy and Gillian Jerome for giving me feedback on various versions of the manuscript.

A special thank you to Michael Turner.

"Thirteen Ways of Looking at a Grey Whale, Ending with a Line from Rilke" was commissioned by the City of Vancouver to mark Vancouver's Greenest City initiative to become the most sustainable city in the World by 2020. I would like to thank *Geist* magazine for first publishing it.

"2010 Handbook for Entering Canada" was written directly after a telephone conversation with Howard White and the poem is for him. Thank you to *The Globe and Mail* and *Geist* magazine for publishing it.

"At Lacy Madden's Grave" was commissioned by the City of Vancouver and the Mountain View Cemetery.

"At the Vancouver Olympics I am Canadian and on TV" is for Geoff Berner.

"In Praise of Female Athletes Who Were Told No" was written after a series of interviews with the fourteen female ski jumpers who sued the Vancouver Organizing Committee for the 2010 Olympic and Paralympic Winter Games, so that they could compete in the 2010 Winter Olympics in Vancouver. The poem is dedicated to Anette Sagen, Jenna Mohr, Lindsey Van, Jessica Jerome, Ulrike Gräßler, Monika Planinc, Marie-Pierre Morin, Karla Keck, Nathalie

De Leeuw, Katherine Willis, Jade Edwards, Zoya Lynch, Charlotte Mitchell and Meaghan Reid, with special thanks to Vic Method, Deedee Corradini, Deborah Folka and Whitney Childers.

"Ink on Paper" is for Daniel Zomparelli and was first published in *Poetry Is Dead*.

"Reading an American Magazine in Vietnam, Perhaps the *New York Times Magazine* and Sometime in 1997" is for Sarah Hill.

"The Avian Flu" is for Eric Nonacs.

"Science Fiction" steals a concept from Ryan Knighton and the poem is for him.

"Fun-Loving Nickleback Policy Machine (with Kittens)" was commissioned by *The Globe and Mail* to mark the end of my tenure as Poet Laureate and I thank the editors for publishing it.

"Normal" is for my daughters Rory and Micah.

"Hands and Pixels," "Conflating Memories While Listening to 'Day in, Day Out' by Billie Holiday" and "Histories" are for Gillian Jerome.

PHOTO: Alex Waterhouse-Hayward

ABOUT THE AUTHOR

Brad Cran served as Poet Laureate for the City of Vancouver from April of 2009 until October of 2011. He published his first book, *The Good Life*, in 2001 and his most recent book, *Hope in Shadows: Stories and Photographs of Vancouver's Downtown Eastside* (with Gillian Jerome), won the City of Vancouver Book Award and has raised over $50,000 for marginalized people in Vancouver's Downtown Eastside. Cran's essay, Notes on a World Class City, defended Vancouver's progressive history and went viral in the lead up to the 2010 Winter Olympic games. He is currently finishing his second book of non-fiction *The Truth About Ronald Reagan: How Movies Changed the World*. *Ink on Paper* is Cran's second book of poetry.